To: _____

From: _____

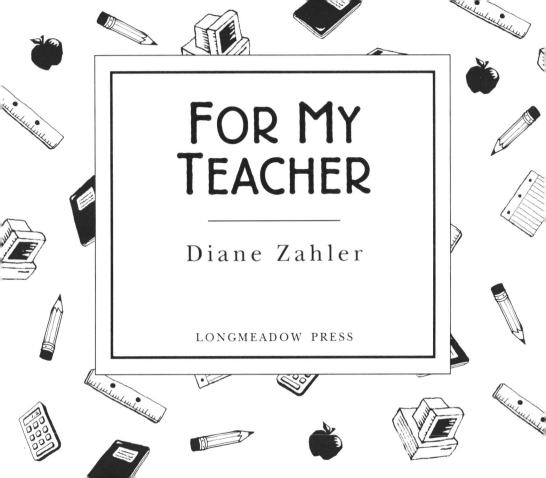

FOR MY TEACHER

Diane Zahler

LONGMEADOW PRESS

Jacket design by Lisa Amoroso
Interior design by Lisa Amoroso
ISBN: 0-681-10021-4
Printed in Singapore
First Edition
0 9 8 7 6 5 4 3 2 1

CONTENTS

Introduction

I believe in the boys and girls, the men and women
of a great tomorrow.

—The Creed of a Teacher

A teacher is often the most important influence in
a person's life—and the most unacknowledged.
How many of us have had our eyes opened to
knowledge by a teacher who was full of enthusiasm, fired with the love of learning? And how
often have we said thank you?

Teachers aren't completely unappreciated, though. For more than two thousand years, great thinkers and writers have been aware of the vital role great teachers play in the development of individuals and of civilization. Here are some of their reflections on teachers and teaching—the skills a teacher needs, the all-important purpose of teaching, the trials and the joys of being a teacher. It's their way—and ours—of saying thank you to the teachers in our lives.

A Teacher's Skills

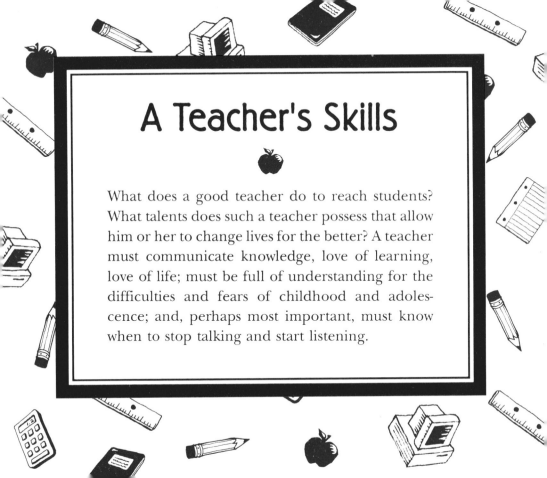

What does a good teacher do to reach students? What talents does such a teacher possess that allow him or her to change lives for the better? A teacher must communicate knowledge, love of learning, love of life; must be full of understanding for the difficulties and fears of childhood and adolescence; and, perhaps most important, must know when to stop talking and start listening.

The secret of teaching is to appear to have known all your life what you learned this afternoon.

—Anonymous

A courage which looks easy and yet is rare; the courage of a teacher repeating day after day the same lessons—the least rewarded of all forms of courage.

—Honoré de Balzac

Men, while teaching, learn.

—Seneca

A teacher who can arouse a feeling for one single good action, for one single good poem, accomplishes more than he who fills our memory with rows and rows of natural objects, classified with name and form.

—*Goethe*

———————————

There's no need to keep your class pin-drop quiet, no need to pass the "white glove" test when you can have a slightly cluttered room lovingly decorated with kids' art and work.

—*Peggy Lewis, Teacher*

The verb "teach" may have every other verb in the dictionary as a synonym. When one teaches well, one does a little of everything: laugh, cry, act, write, live, die—the list is endless.

—*Len DeAngelis, Teacher*

Teaching is an instinctual art, mindful of potential, craving of realizations, a pausing, seamless process.

—*A. Bartlett Giamatti,*
University President

Whene'er you lecture, be concise: the soul
Takes in short maxims, and retains them whole;
But pour in water when the vessel's filled,
It simply dribbles over and is spilled.

—*Horace*

These words—*dedication, motivation, enthusiasm*—I know they are used all the time, but they are real qualities, and they are necessary to be effective in a classroom.

—*Cynthia Fremont, Teacher*

FOR MY TEACHER

He that has found a way to keep a child's spirit easy, active, and free, and yet at the same time to restrain him from many things he has a mind to, and to draw him to things that are uneasy to him, has, in my opinion, got the true secret of education.

—*John Locke*

I maintain, in truth
That with a smile we should instruct our youth.
Be very gentle when we have to blame,
And not put them in fear of virtue's name.

—*Molière*

To know how to suggest is the great art of teaching. To attain it we must be able to guess what will interest; we must learn to read the childish soul as we might a piece of music.

—*H. F. Amiel*

Mr. Rhind is very kind,
He goes to kirk on Sunday.
He prays to God to give him strength
to skelp the bairns on Monday.

—*Anonymous*

You have to be mother, father, preacher, counselor, friend and disciplinarian all in one. Somewhere you have to slip in the role of teacher.

—Karen Cahill, Teacher

The best teacher of children . . . is one who is essentially childlike.

—H. L. Mencken

The secret of education lies in respecting the pupil.

—Ralph Waldo Emerson

Educators should be chosen not merely for their special qualifications, but more for their personality and their character, because we teach more by what we are than by what we teach.

—William James Durant

A child, however educated, is still untaught if by his teaching we have not emphasized his individual character, if we have not strengthened his will and its guide and guardian, the mind.

—David Starr Jordan

One looks back with appreciation to the brilliant teachers, but with gratitude to those who touched our human feelings. The curriculum is so much necessary raw material, but warmth is a vital element for the growing plant and for the soul of the child.

—Carl Jung

As between a teacher who knows little but can incite in his pupils a love of learning and one who knows a great deal and has not the power to incite that love of learning, I prefer the former. He is by far the more valuable of the two.

—Champ Clark

Tell me and I'll forget. Show me, and I may not remember. Involve me, and I'll understand.

—*American Indian saying*

———

In seeking knowledge, the first step is silence, the second listening, the third remembering, the fourth practicing, and the fifth—teaching others.

—*Ibn Gabirol*

———

When the schoolmaster gentle is and sweet,
The boys will play at leap-frog in the street.

—*Gulistan*

Education is a painful, continual and difficult work to be done by kindness, by watching, by warning, by precept, and by praise; but above all, by example.

—John Ruskin

Good teaching is ¼th preparation and ¾ths theatre.

—Gail Godwin

Human beings are full of emotion, and the teacher who knows how to use it will have dedicated learners.

—Leon Lessinger, Dean

A good teacher, like a good entertainer, first must hold his audience's attention. Then he can teach his lesson.

—*John Henrik Clarke*

I have always felt that the true text book for the pupil is his teacher.

—*Mahatma Gandhi*

One of the important duties of a teacher is to keep a roomful of live wires grounded.

—*Anonymous*

A Teacher's Purpose

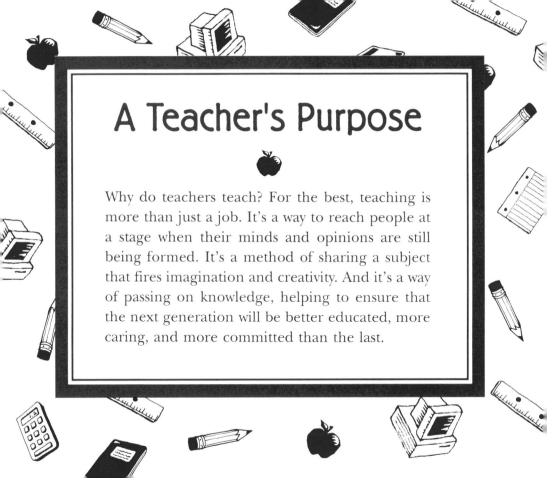

Why do teachers teach? For the best, teaching is more than just a job. It's a way to reach people at a stage when their minds and opinions are still being formed. It's a method of sharing a subject that fires imagination and creativity. And it's a way of passing on knowledge, helping to ensure that the next generation will be better educated, more caring, and more committed than the last.

Education is not the filling of a pail, but the lighting of a fire.

—William Butler Yeats

At the beginning I was only a little mass of possibilities. It was my teacher who unfolded and developed them.

—Helen Keller

The object of teaching a child is to enable him to get along without his teacher.

—Elbert Hubbard

To strengthen children's minds and to cultivate graces, to build strong bodies and develop loveliness of character, are astonishing privileges. No king or head of state has a more noble calling.

—Raymond S. Moore

The foundation of every state is the education of its youth.

—Diogenes

A teacher affects eternity; he can never tell where his influence stops.

—Henry Adams

All the world over there is a realisation that only through right education can a better order of society be built up.

—*Jawaharlal Nehru*

Everyone who remembers his own education remembers teachers, not methods and techniques. The teacher is the kingpin of the educational system.

—*Sidney Hook*

Teachers are greater benefactors than parents.

—*Pope Xystus I*

An education isn't how much you have committed to memory, or even how much you know. It's being able to differentiate between what you *do* know and what you don't. It's knowing where to go to find out what you need to know. And it's knowing how to use the information once you get it.

—*Thomas Henry Huxley*

———

The real test of education is how we live as individuals and as groups. If we cherish hatred and antagonism, our education has failed. If we learn how to love, our training has been truly successful.

—*Dr. Frederick Mayer*

Character development is the great, if not the sole, aim of education.

—William James O'Shea

Teachers, who educate children, deserve more honor than parents, who merely gave them birth; for the latter provided mere life, while the former ensure a good life.

—Aristotle

Education is the torch that destroys the fear in the heart of man.

—James Malof

The entire object of true education is to make people not merely do the right thing, but enjoy the right things; not merely industrious, but to love industry; not merely learned, but to love knowledge; not merely pure, but to love purity; not merely just, but to hunger and thirst after justice.

—John Ruskin

The first duty of a lecturer—to hand you after an hour's discourse a nugget of pure truth to wrap up between the pages of your notebooks and keep on the mantelpiece for ever.

—Virginia Woolf

A school should be the most beautiful place in every town and village—so beautiful that the punishment for undutiful children should be that they should be debarred from going to school the following day.

—*Oscar Wilde*

The essence of our effort to see that every child has a chance must be to assure each an equal opportunity, not to become equal, but to become different—to realize whatever unique potential of body, mind and spirit he or she possesses.

—*John Rischer,*
Dean

Whoever teaches his son also teaches his son's son—and so on to the end of man's generations.

—Talmud: <u>Kiddishun</u>

The whole art of teaching is only the art of awakening the natural curiosity of young minds for the purpose of satisfying it afterwards.

—Anatole France

The aim is to get kids to make their education rather than receive it. To start right away nurturing rather than destroying the self, the spirit.

—Sam Bush, Teacher

Teachers can save lives as surely and successfully as doctors.

—*Eliot Wigginton,*
Teacher of the Year

Education today, more than ever before, must see clearly the dual objectives: education for living and educating for making a living.

—*James Mason Wood*

If you think education is expensive—try ignorance.

—*Derek Bok*

What nobler employment, or more valuable to the state, than that of the man who instructs the rising generation?

—Cicero

———————

The true aim of every one who aspires to be a teacher should be, not to impart his own opinions, but to kindle minds.

—Frederick William Robinson

———————

The teacher is one who makes two ideas grow where only one grew before.

—Elbert Hubbard

The school should always have as its aim that the young man leave it as a harmonious personality, not as a specialist.

—*Albert Einstein*

Histories make men wise; poems, witty; the mathematics, subtle; natural philosophy, deep; morals, grave; logic and rhetoric, able to contend.

—*Sir Francis Bacon*

A human being is not, in any proper sense, a human being till he is educated.

—*Horace Mann*

Education enables youth to light tomorrow with today; thus the teacher is the servant of the future—of the day after tomorrow.

—*Eugene P. Bertin*

———————

' **T**is education forms the common mind;
Just as the twig is bent the tree's inclined.

—*Alexander Pope*

———————

You should have education so that you won't have to look up to people; and then more education so that you will be wise enough not to look down on people.

—*M. L. Boren*

A Teacher's Trials

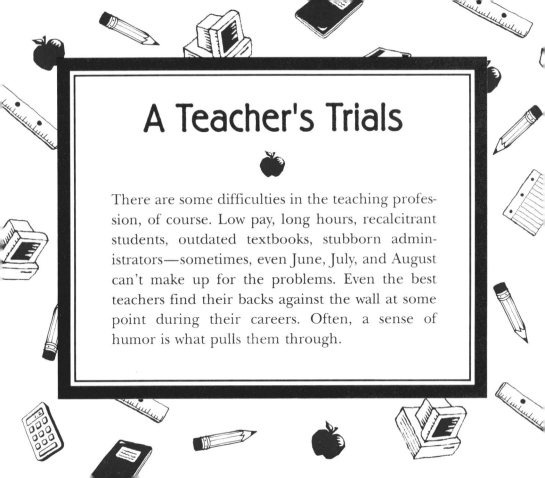

There are some difficulties in the teaching profession, of course. Low pay, long hours, recalcitrant students, outdated textbooks, stubborn administrators—sometimes, even June, July, and August can't make up for the problems. Even the best teachers find their backs against the wall at some point during their careers. Often, a sense of humor is what pulls them through.

A teacher is a person who faces a bunch of desperadoes with her back to the wall and no gun in her hand.

—Anonymous

H ousework is a breeze. Cooking is a pleasant diversion. Putting up a retaining wall is a lark. But teaching is like climbing a mountain.

—Fawn M. Brodie

M arks and grades—originally the measure of learning—have become a substitute for learning. Students work for grades—not knowledge.

—Jesse S. Nirenberg

Grave is the Master's look; his forehead wears
Thick rows of wrinkles, prints of worrying cares:
Uneasy lie the heads of all that rule,
His worst of all whose kingdom is a school.

— *Oliver Wendell Holmes, Sr.*

The worst possible economy is to build a million-dollar school and then staff it with $3000-a-year teachers.

— *Andrew D. Holt*

The schools ain't what they used to be and never was.

— *Will Rogers*

It has been said that we have not had the three R's in America, we had the six R's: remedial readin', remedial 'ritin' and remedial 'rithmetic.

—*Robert M. Hutchins,*
University Chancellor

If the student fails to learn the teacher fails to teach.

—*Anonymous*

We need more materials and more time. The curriculum is handed down, but we need time to adapt it to the level of the kids with the books we have available. Time to plan and develop is not respected.

—*Marilyn Moore, Teacher*

I was, but am no more, thank God—a school teacher—I dreamed last night I was teaching again—that's the only bad dream that ever afflicts my sturdy conscience.

—*D. H. Lawrence*

Our schools are still set up as though every mother were at home all day and the whole family needed the summer to get the crops in.

—*Sidney Callahan*

Teaching is not a lost art, but the regard for it is a lost tradition.

—*Jacques Barzun*

The electronic environment makes an information level outside the schoolroom that is far higher than the information level inside the schoolroom. . . . The child knows that in going to school he is in a sense interrupting his education.

—H. Marshall McLuhan

More people than ever before are graduated but not educated.

—Robert G. Gunderson

The trouble with schools is that they fill kids with knowledge but don't teach them how to use it.

—Bill Stepien, Teacher

Values have changed, and the means to attain the changed goals have changed. Education does not seem to be, to these kids, the way to achieve those things important to them.

—Jim Aufderheide, Teacher

A teacher's lot is not a happy one; the worst-behaved schoolchild usually has the best attendance record.

—Anonymous

Schools are now asked to do what people used to ask God to do.

—Jerome Cramer

A Teacher's Joys

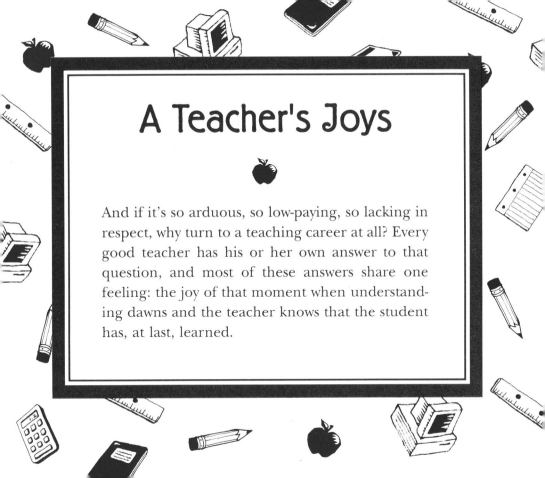

And if it's so arduous, so low-paying, so lacking in respect, why turn to a teaching career at all? Every good teacher has his or her own answer to that question, and most of these answers share one feeling: the joy of that moment when understanding dawns and the teacher knows that the student has, at last, learned.

My heart is singing for joy this morning. A miracle has happened! The light of understanding has shone upon my little pupil's mind, and behold, all things are changed!

—Annie Sullivan

I came and I stayed because of the spark I see in the students' eyes. I see future architects, musicians, lawyers, and teachers—dynamic, multifaceted people with dreams.

—Laura Charles, Teacher

No other job in the world could possibly dispossess one so completely as this job of teaching. . . . It cuts right into your being: essentially, it takes over your spirit. It drags it out from where it would hide.

—Sylvia Ashton-Warner

The job centers around a fascination with kids. And for all the kids I've taught, I can hardly think of two who are really alike.

—Allen Rondo, Teacher

"But then from Study will no Comforts rise?"
Yes! such as studious Minds alone can prize;
Comforts, yea!—Joys ineffable they find,
Who seek the prouder Pleasures of the Mind:
The Soul, collected in those happy hours,
Then makes her efforts, then enjoys her powers;
And in those seasons feels herself repaid,
For Labours past and Honours long delay'd.

—*George Crabbe*

———————

There is no chalk dust on the sleeve of my soul.

—*John Barth*

I am a teacher. There is no magic here. I do not walk on water. I do not part the sea. I just love children.

—*Marva Collins, Teacher*

Here lies a teacher. That's all I ever was, that's all I am, that's the one thing I really do well.

—*Harry Edwards, Teacher*

It is a luxury to learn; but the luxury of learning is not to be compared with the luxury of teaching.

—*R. D. Hitchcock*

I feel good about what I do. I enjoy 30 different personalities each hour. . . . I've found my niche in life with teaching.

—*Brenda Ring, Teacher*

We are teachers—heirs of an honored heritage and recipients of a high calling. . . . We are teachers—dreamers who glimpse tomorrow's triumphs if only through today's tears. We are teachers who care passionately about what really matters.

—*Daniel J. Estes, Teacher*

Why do I stay? Because of the magic, the joy, and the celebrations. Because the growth and development of the kids is the growth and development of me. It is my way to make the world more beautiful.

—Judith Shively, Teacher

My greatest satisfaction comes when my students find the success they never thought they could have.

—Addie Rhodes Lee,
Teacher of the Year

A pupil receives but a fifth of the reward that accrues to the teacher.

—*Midrash:*
Song of Songs Rabbah

———————

Teachers should be held in the highest honor. They are the allies of legislators; they have agency in the prevention of crime; they aid in regulating the atmosphere, whose incessant action and pressure cause the life-blood to circulate, and to return pure and healthful to the heart of the nation.

—*Lydia Howard Sigourney*

Teaching grows more beautiful to me—*teaching!*—who am I that I can *teach?* I feel more and more after the year's work how responsible I am for what I teach.

Mary Graves, Teacher

My teacher is so near to me that I scarcely think of myself apart from her. . . . All the best of me belongs to her—there is not a talent, or an aspiration or a joy in me that has not been awakened by her loving touch.

—Helen Keller

A Teacher's Worst Nightmare

Of course, everyone should have a bad experience with a teacher at some point. The grade school ogre who demanded utter silence at all times, the high school mumbler whose class was shocked awake each day by the bell, the professor whose favorite grade was not A, B, C, or D. . . . Wouldn't those teachers be horrified to know how vivid an impression they made on their students?

My education was so sound that I know hardly anything.

—*Ronald Mackenzie*

There is less flogging in our great schools than formerly, but then less is learned there; so that what the boys get at one end they lose at the other.

—*Samuel Johnson*

Nothing in education is so astonishing as the amount of ignorance it accumulates in the form of inert facts.

—*Henry Adams*

The vanity of teaching often tempteth a man to forget he is a blockhead.

—Lord Halifax

———————

Schoolmasters and parents exist to be grown out of.

—John Wolfenden

———————

    Seven pupils in the class
of Professor Callias
Listen silent while he drawls.—
Three are benches, four are walls.

—Henry Van Dyke

Soap and education are not as sudden as a massacre, but they are more deadly in the long run.

—Mark Twain

Teaching may hasten learning; it may also block it or kill it outright, or sometimes just render it comatose for years.

—James Harvey Robinson

Teaching is the fine art of imparting knowledge without possessing it.

—Anonymous

Teachers are overworked and underpaid. True, it is an exacting and exhausting business, this damming up the flood of human potentialities.

—George B. Leonard

———————

A teacher is a person who knows all the answers, but only when she asks the questions.

—Anonymous

———————

Education is an admirable thing, but it is well to remember from time to time that nothing that is worth knowing can be taught.

—Oscar Wilde